Brain Training for Volleyball

A Guide to Teaching Focus, Leadership and a Winning Attitude

Stephanie Schleuder

Printed in the United States of America

First Printing, 2017

ISBN 978-0-9989765-1-8

Written by Stephanie Schleuder
Edited by Don Patterson

Published by The Art of Coaching Volleyball, LLC
3720 SW 141st Avenue, Suite 209
Beaverton, OR 97005

www.theartofcoachingvolleyball.com

Table of Contents

Introduction

As a young coach, I believed there were two indispensable keys to athletic success. First, a coach needed elite athletes who were well-conditioned, with superior skills. Second, these athletes had to be able to effectively execute specific tactics and strategies as prescribed in game situations. My woeful assumptions came as a 24-year old who had just been hired as the head volleyball and head basketball coach at the University of Alabama. I'm more than slightly embarrassed to admit that the many intrinsic aspects of coaching that I barely considered or knew anything about included such things as mental skills, personal motivation, team chemistry or resilience. Leadership, which we all believe is crucial to success, was something I thought people were born with, not a personal attribute coaches could develop or enhance through thoughtful mentoring. At that time, I gave little consideration to how those aspects of human behavior could sway an athlete's or a team's ability to be successful. More important, I didn't recognize how influential they could be in the personal growth of each player. It was the dawn of collegiate athletics for women, and I obviously had lots to learn.

Fast forward 40 years and my beliefs are dramatically different. I certainly don't claim to have all the answers. Over time, motivated by frustration, the desire to win and a sincere interest in mentoring young people, I have developed some effective strategies to help athletes mature and succeed – as athletes, as members of a team and, ultimately, as human beings. I've been fortunate to learn from many great coaches as well as people active in psychology, child development and business. I even got meaningful mentoring from an indigenous shaman.

With each passing year, I found myself becoming more and more passionate about finding ways to help athletes through a process of self-discovery and personal growth. I was an active learner right along with them, frequently battling my own preconceived assumptions. Increasingly, I came to comprehend how athletic success encompassed WAY more than a goal of having elite athletes with superior skills and implementing effective tactics with sound strategies. Now, I firmly believe that it is frequently not the most talented athletes or teams that win. The best teams and athletes often have an array of tools and competencies, unrelated to their athletic prowess. These enable them to connect, problem-solve and persevere in the face of adversity.

X's and O's vs. Intangibles

It seems to me that we coaches have a "focus" problem. I have asked many professional golfers if their success is related to physical or mental skills. They readily say that it's 90% mental, maybe more. When I've asked volleyball coaches what percentage of their players' success is mental, I get everything from 60% to 85%. The next logical question is how much time is spent on developing physical skills vs. mental skills? Nervous laughter invariably follows that question, and this brings me to our focus problem. Almost without exception, volleyball coaches reserve little time for working on mental skills or intangibles. I believe ignoring or discounting training for interpersonal and mental skills unnecessarily increases the risk of frustration, failure and disharmony among your team members.

So much of coaching education centers on the physical aspects of teaching skills, physical training and how to conduct competitive, efficient and effective practices. There is always a coach introducing a new skill or a new way to perform an old skill. In recent years, it has become more common to see coaching clinics cover aspects of mental training or group dynamics. Yet those sessions rarely draw huge crowds.

My primary goal in writing this book is to make the case that success and winning are often determined more by what people refer to as the intangibles than by the X's and O's. Most simply defined, these intangibles are methods and strategies designed to promote personal awareness and growth with the goal of enhancing performance.

The Intangibles that Matter

Coaching is analogous to putting together a huge jigsaw puzzle. It's a multi-faceted process. Introducing new concepts to your athletes requires finding a way to hook them into the process. They have to understand how it can help them.

I have tried to organize the concepts in this book into an easy-to-use format that includes worksheets and suggestions for the coach. Here is a brief overview of the strategies presented:

- 10 Steps to Improving a Player's Personal Motivation

- Coaching Captains to be Leaders

- Teaching Your Players to be Leaders

- Team Chemistry: How to Mold a Good Team into a Great Team

- 6 Keys to Developing Competitive Team Spirit

- Managing Behaviors: Strategies to Help Players Monitor Themselves

- Dealing with the Doldrums

- Defeating Distractions: Strategies to Help Players Stay Focused

- Bitching: The Greatest Threat to Athletic Progress

- Trust Building Strategies to Promote Team Bonding

- The Celebration Phenomenon: Changing the Energy Level of Your Team

10 Steps to Improving a Player's Personal Motivation

Inspiring your players is mostly about educating them on how they can best inspire themselves. Here's a step-by-step guide that will help you do just that.

Let's face it, the never-ending pursuit to capture the secret of motivation can be a nightmare journey. How often have you heard a coach say they were struggling to motivate their players? Or maybe you've listened to honest players confide that they are stressed about their own personal lack of motivation. Better yet, the team offers a "helpful" explanation for their lack of enthusiasm before a big game, citing the coach's inability to give a good motivational pre-game speech. Good luck with that one!

I have come to believe that we, as coaches, are making a mistake by thinking this whole motivation issue is our problem. The reality is, only a small part of it is our problem. I think we have to challenge and educate our players about their own role in motivation.

Step 1

Discuss motivation with your players so they develop a better understanding of it. Encourage your players to take notes, and cover the following points:

- Motivation is specific to the individual, so your setter may be motivated by something very different than one of your middle blockers. Extrinsic motivation – things like pre-game speeches, incentives, bribes, threats or fear-based motivation – might work for some while others may not respond or may even resent these methods.

- Athletes are all different people with different values, feelings, strengths, weaknesses and goals. It's counterproductive for a coach to treat all players the same.

- Young people today have grown up in a society that generally spoon feeds them. Rarely are they asked to figure things out for themselves. I think this ends up being a real disservice to our athletes. Present this exercise as a "journey" and an opportunity to learn about self-discovery and personal introspection.

- Extrinsic motivation doesn't last and doesn't promote personal growth. I don't want robots; I want people who think, feel and solve problems. So don't expect rousing pre-game speeches designed to fire you up or bribes for a big win. The goal is for motivation to come from within you.

Step 2
Help your players help themselves

- One of the biggest keys to teaching players how to motivate themselves is to help them first discover what's really important to them, then to identify how they can be even more fulfilled. When people realize their potential, they generally feel good about themselves.

- As a coach, your goal is to help them be successful in this journey. For this to be effective, trust, honesty, integrity, communication and mutual respect will be valuable assets. It will be a two-way street.

- Important note for coaches: Listen to your players and value their feelings. Playing head games with players is dishonest and counterproductive. Trust me, this behavior will come back to bite you!

Step 3
Part 1 of the Personal Motivation Worksheet

Before you go any further, ask the players to complete part 1 of this worksheet. Encourage them to take their time and give honest, thoughtful responses. Speeding carelessly through this will doom the entire process.

This worksheet is for each player's personal use, so the information doesn't need to be shared unless the player chooses to share it.

Worksheet - Part 1

1. What part of your work, personal life, and/or school do you like best? Why?

2. What don't you like about your situation (work, personal life, school)? Why?

3. Are you happy and/or content? If you answer no, what would you want to change?

Step 4
Introduce the definition of motivation

Definition: Motivation is "knowing what it is that really excites you and that you value, and doing it."

Here are some tips that will help players figure this out:

- When you have free time, what do you sit and think about? (e.g., boyfriends/girlfriends, your team, vacation.)

- It takes no energy to think about it.

- People who have faced death or a close call report saying to themselves, "This is what I want to spend time doing."

- It doesn't matter what other people say or think as long as you like it and have a passion for it.

- Some people need to give themselves permission to be happy. You have choices. You deserve to be happy.

- Figure out what percentage of the time you are doing things that truly make you happy. If the percentage is low, ask yourself what needs to change so it will increase.

Step 5

Part 2 of the Personal Motivation Worksheet

Worksheet - Part 2

1. Describe what excites you and what you would like to be able to do all the time.

2. To be happy, what percent of your time do you realistically need to be able to do what you really like?

Step 6

Help your players understand that they must accept complete and total responsibility for their own situation

Here are two questions to ask them that will assist with this process:

1. "Do you want to be here?" This can be scary for a coach. I've asked this of players who have been pressured by parents (or someone else) to play, and it's a tough question. But it never ends up being fulfilling for them unless it's their desire. Sometimes they just have to be given permission to make their own decision.

2. Are you playing because you like and value volleyball and it excites you? On a scale of 1 to 10, how much do you like volleyball? The answer to this question is important. If you like something a lot, generating motivation is much easier.

Next, encourage your players to take action if they are feeling discouraged, burned out, trapped or angry. These feelings tend to surface when someone feels they have no control, so it's your job as the coach to remind them of the following:

1. They have choices. If they aren't happy, they can work to change the situation or they can quit.

2. Working at something to get good is difficult, but remember this: The world usually wants you to do something you don't want to do or something you don't care about. It's up to you.

Step 7
Part 3 of the Personal Motivation Worksheet

Worksheet - Part 3

1. Have you committed yourself totally to doing what really excites you?

   - If the answer is no: What is keeping you from this commitment?
   - If the answer is yes: How have you committed yourself to doing what really excites you?

Step 8

Have more discussion about making a commitment to what excites you and cover the following points:

- Dare to be true to your own feeling and commit yourself to something that you want to do. This is hard! Everyone tries to tell you what you should do or what you should be (should = shame).

- Don't let someone stop you. It's risky and scary to commit to something that truly excites you, but this is what allows for personal growth.

- Change is hard and uncomfortable, but you will adapt. The body doesn't adapt because it's comfortable; it adapts because it's trying to keep from being uncomfortable. (e.g., If you rub your finger repeatedly, callouses will develop so you won't get blisters.)

- Wish for the ability to learn, not talent. Talented people often don't know how to learn because they count on talent. You all know someone who is brilliant and never had to study to get A's. Some of the best coaches in the world were average players who are able to teach others how to learn because they had to learn.

Step 9
Part 4 of the Personal Motivation Worksheet

Worksheet - Part 4

1. What do you have to be able to do/change in order to do what really excites you?

   - Physically
   - Emotionally
   - Mentally

2. What things have made it difficult or kept you from being successful at doing what you want?

3. Develop a plan to accomplish your goals. Include a prioritized daily schedule of activities like practice, games, workouts, studying, attending to personal chores and social time.

Step 10
Define and discuss discipline

Definition: Discipline is knowing what it is that you need to do, and not always wanting to do it but doing it anyway.

Key points to discuss:

- Here is the reality check! We can't do what we want to do all the time.

- You usually have to do some things you don't want to do or enjoy as much to be able to do what you enjoy (e.g., homework, library research, conditioning, practice, lifting weights).

- Think about (or write down) a personal discipline situation you have had recently. Was it something you needed to do or is it something someone told you that you should do? Why? Does it fit in your plan for happiness? What would you rather be doing? How does this fit into your overall plan?

- Personal discipline is an act of will. For example, if a friend asks you to go to a party when you know you need to get to bed early, you can respond:

    1. "No, coach will be mad if she finds out." (No responsibility for your action.)

    2. "No, sleep is important because volleyball is my first priority." (You just took responsibility for your action.)

- Is there one (or more) person to whom you have trouble saying no? Why and what can you do about it?

A Final Thought

Remind your players that they aren't going to be 100 percent motivated 100 percent of the time. Motivation comes and goes. That's normal. You can't be perfect.

Personal Motivation Worksheet

1. What part of your work, personal life, and/or school do you like best? Why?

2. What don't you like about your situation (work, personal life, school)? Why?

3. Are you happy and/or content? If you answer no, what would you want to change?

4. Describe what excites you and what you would like to be able to do all the time.

5. To be happy, what percent of your time do you realistically need to be able to do what you really like?

6. Have you committed yourself totally to doing what really excites you?

   - If the answer is no: What is keeping you from this commitment?
   - If the answer is yes: How have you committed yourself to doing what really excites you?

7. What do you have to be able to do/change to do what really excites you?

   - Physically, emotionally, mentally

8. What things have made it difficult or kept you from being successful at doing what you want?

9. Develop a plan to accomplish your goals. Include a prioritized daily schedule of activities like practice, games, workouts, studying, attending to personal chores and social time.

Selecting Captains

There are myriad ways captains can be selected: nomination by the players, election by players, selection by the coach or a combination of methods.

It seems important to have player input so they will feel an investment in the results. Once the players have a better understanding of leadership, they will likely give more valuable input to the process. I personally believe it is an advantage to have more than one captain. If you have a strong core of returning players, it can be a good thing to select captains in the spring or summer. That gives you time to begin coaching them to be effective leaders.

10 Keys to Training Captains

1. Your players are inexperienced young adults who have little or no training in communication and public speaking. Don't expect miracles without engaging captains in extensive training and discussion.

2. Captains will have natural fears about taking on a role where they are expected to communicate individually with a teammate or with a group of teammates. Let them know this is OK.

3. One of the first sessions should deal with communication. Be sure to emphasize the importance of listening and observing teammates.

4. Emphasize the role of the captain as one of honor and responsibility.

5. Captains should form a "team within a team." Each captain can have different responsibilities that match their individual personality and leadership skills.

6. The coach should lead extensive discussion of leadership principles such as communicating the expectation message, mental preparation, delegation of responsibility and group and personal ethics (integrity). All of this leads to the overriding principle that a leader assumes responsibility for the performance of others and the outcome of the quest. Learning what the team needs is critical.

7. Do not impose coaching responsibilities on the captains. Coaches should retain responsibility for personnel or playing time choices, game strategy and training regimens.

8. There will always be players who are defiant, resentful, distracted or unmotivated. Coaches may or may not be successful in dealing with these players. Captains have a unique capacity to deal with these individuals on a peer-to-peer basis. The principles of duty to the team and the integrity of the captain's position are critical to being able to deal with these individuals.

9. A team is a social organization. It has a complex social structure, a chain of command and a variety of skill sets distributed among its participants. There are mood swings from euphoria to bitter deflation. The captains must understand that they should rally the team in times of despair, creating a culture of resilience. With the ability to be resilient comes growing confidence in the ability to succeed.

10. Before the season, the coach must determine what the team's biggest obstacles will be and shape the priorities for the captains. For example, will it be overcoming previous lack of success and lack of confidence, or will it be living up to expectations of previous success?

Teaching Your Players to be Leaders

Fewer and fewer young athletes are embracing leadership roles, so it's your job as the coach to show them the way.

A prominent topic among coaches today is the lack of leadership we see in today's athletes. Why aren't more players stepping up and taking charge? One theory is that the explosion of adult-run youth sports programs has drastically reduced the number of players who take leadership roles.

In the good old days, kids naturally developed leadership skills because they picked their own teams, decided the rules, determined the lineups, officiated their games and learned about problem solving from handling conflicts themselves.

Research tells us that young people today are often more concerned with fitting in than standing out. These relatively new circumstances create challenges for coaches, who often implore athletes to demonstrate leadership, then get frustrated when they don't.

Finally, while all athletes have been coached to perform skills, it's likely that many of today's athletes have received little or no training related to leadership.

What is the athlete's perception of leadership?

I believe that awareness is a key concept to be tackled before a coach can make any significant progress toward changing or enhancing both the mental and physical skills of athletes. Therefore, it's important for coaches to explore their athletes' knowledge and conceptual understanding of leadership.

One way this can be accomplished is by having players complete a short questionnaire and then participating in a coach-led discussion. I find it's best to give them the questionnaire as an assignment so they can be more thoughtful in considering their answers. Tell them they will be sharing their answers with the rest of the team. On the day of the discussion, have one of the athletes write all of their responses on a chalkboard. Next, have the team develop one or more statements that represent a team consensus for each item.

Questionnaire for Team Members

1. Define leadership.

2. List three people you respect for their leadership ability (from any phase of your life).

3. List characteristics of these effective leaders.

4. How do effective leaders influence your performance?

5. Do effective leaders influence your self-esteem? If so, how?

6. Name some rewards of being a team leader?

7. What are risks associated with being a team leader?

8. Name some characteristics of great groups/teams?

9. What do you think is the best way to select team leaders/captains?

Define Personal Leadership Styles

Athletes will likely need assistance/coaching to clearly define the type of leadership they want to provide to the team. It's important for players to understand that their leadership style will likely be significantly influenced by their personality. The Myers Briggs Personality Assessment is an excellent tool to help players better understand themselves. A great deal of information is available on this website:

www.myersbriggs.org/my-mbti-personality-type/ take-the-mbti-instrument/

The Myers Briggs Assessment is often available through school counselors or campus resource centers. After everyone receives their results, schedule a meeting to discuss them. This is a perfect offseason or preseason activity. My experience is that players love it.

Assign like personality styles to a group – discuss how their style influences their interpersonal and group interactions (behaviors). Have each group list pitfalls and positive aspects of their leadership style. Talk about how the behaviors connected to their personality style can be an asset to the team.

Cultivating Leadership Opportunities for Non-Captains

It's essential for non-captains to understand the intricacies of effective leadership. Even though they're not the designated captain(s), they can contribute valuable leadership both on and off the court. This is a critical aspect of getting non-captains to take part in team leadership. For example, the coach can assign an appropriate leadership role to some or all non-captains. Captains will likely have more extensive roles, but the rest of the leadership roles may incorporate elements of the list below. I used this for a number of years and found it effective in keeping players engaged and vocal. In addition to giving players clear-cut assignments, it increases court awareness and connects them to their teammates. Here are some examples with possible responsibilities:

Team Chemistry:
How to Mold a Good Team into a Great Team

"The way a team plays as a whole determines its success. You may have the greatest bunch of individual stars in the world, but if they don't play together, the club won't be worth a dime."
                                        -Babe Ruth

All coaches try to figure out how to get the most out of their team. Successful, veteran coaches understand the importance of the team environment in sustained success. Some spend countless hours stewing over how to corral that elusive, magical component of good team chemistry. If we achieve it, it's likely that it will propel the team to an incredible season. And chemistry can help your team exceed expectations even when you don't have the most skilled players. I've seen it happen to my teams on more than one occasion. Even though we were decidedly less skilled and less athletic, we played with an ease and intensity devoid of stress that translated into a determination and desire to play for each other – to support each other. You could see it and feel it and I firmly believe it wasn't an accident that it happened. We worked to make it happen. I'm not claiming that it's always possible to reach this point – there are lots of moving parts – but you're much more likely to get there if you have a basic understanding of team chemistry and a plan.

What is team chemistry?

It's hard to definitively explain team chemistry, but there are typically some common interpersonal components. These can occur naturally among team members or they may need to be nurtured. That's where the coach comes in. You can decide whether to share this list with your players. Hopefully, the process described here will stimulate discussion that leads them to their own discoveries, which are always more valuable.

Using this list as a barometer for progress, you can make sure each point is somehow incorporated into your discussions with players. Here are 8 seminal characteristics of good team chemistry:

1. No drama. Women are notorious for making a big deal about a lot of things ... boyfriend problems, interpersonal issues with a teammate, problems with the coach, decisions about starters and playing time, being "slighted" by an innocent remark and distracting teammates with trivial personal issues. You get the idea. Teammates or coaches may have to tactfully address this. Drama has to become unacceptable.

2. Expect mistakes. The coach believes and actively accepts mistakes as part of the learning process

while clarifying acceptable (smart) risks. For example, when to "go for it" with a big swing at the ball as opposed to being more deliberate with a poor set.

3. Mutual desire to support each other on and off the court. Players reject divisive behavior like gossip and allowing "clicks" to develop and instead work to develop trusting, inclusive relationships.

4. Sense of humor. Players and coaches should feel free to laugh (appropriately) about funny things that happen in the gym and on the court. Many coaches need to lighten up!

5. Mutual respect. All people connected to the team matter as an important part of the puzzle.

6. Embrace the challenge. Framing or re-framing important competitions as opportunities can reduce players' feelings of fear, apprehension and nervousness.

7. Selfless and resilient. Rather than playing for individual accolades, members of the team play for and support each other, especially in tough situations. For players, the focus should be on the team, not themselves.

8. Convictions, beliefs and self-confidence become stronger than doubts. Players don't suppress

emotions, they become aware of them and use them in a positive way. Joyless, stoic, poker-faced play rarely produces long-term positive results. It inhibits the critical energetic interconnectedness among players.

How do you build team chemistry?

I'd like to share my approach to this goal. What follows is a program designed to enhance the personal growth of both players and coaches, which will in turn set the stage for fostering sustained, positive team chemistry. It's really important for players and coaches to embrace and adopt all aspects of this work. As the coach, you are part of the team. If you don't engage, the players will see your hypocrisy immediately and your work will be less than fruitful.

A guiding light

Many years ago I came across a book, *The Four Agreements*. It was written by don Miguel Ruiz and published in 1997. In essence, the book describes a code of conduct (four agreements) that it says can transform our lives into a more happy and fulfilling experience. It talks about self-limiting beliefs and actions that rob us of joy and create needless anguish. The part about self-limiting beliefs hit me like a sledge hammer; that's a huge hurdle for coaches.

I bought the book on the spot. It's only 138 pages, but it has a wealth of insight into human behavior, especially the beliefs and actions that stifle us. I asked my players to buy it and read it and told them we would be using it during preseason training with our journals. We had four 90-minute evening sessions. It was worth every minute of time players spent doing the individual work and then having team discussion of the "four agreements."

The worksheet was used for individual work and guided group discussion. (We broke up into small groups, then had discussions with the entire team.)

Later in the season, we revisited the subject. This was especially important if we were struggling. I have adapted the book's language in the points that follow so it's more applicable to players.

Agreement 1
Be impeccable with your word

- Speak with integrity. Say only what you mean. Avoid using words to put yourself down or to gossip about others. Use the power of your words for speaking truthfully and with respect. You will only receive a negative idea if your mind is fertile ground for that idea. For example, negative self-talk inhibits your personal growth or skill development. Repeating gossip or saying something meant to diminish someone else is very divisive.

- Your words reveal who you are. Your word is pure magic (giving, sharing and respecting); misuse of your word is black magic (destructive and deceitful). Your intent/goal is powerful and it is the key. Check your intent when you are in doubt or when you grapple with a difficult issue — is it pure or impure? For example, you think a teammate criticized you so you tell another player what they said to you. Are you looking for sympathy or condemnation of that player? Pure intent would be to personally and calmly talk to the player rather than a third party.

- Your word is a force. It is the power you have to express and communicate, to think, and thereby to create the events in your life. It is the most powerful gift we have as humans. It should not be used against ourselves or others.

- Impeccability means "without sin." (Latin: pecatus means sin; im means without) You go against yourself when you judge or blame yourself for anything. When you are impeccable, you take responsibility for your actions, but you do not judge or blame yourself. Being impeccable with your word is the correct use of your energy; it means you use your energy for truth and respect.

Coaches should pay special attention to this one. Many players really are hard on themselves. Gently make that unacceptable. And remember, coaches who yell, belittle or embarrass players for mistakes are doing them a disservice. Players don't go out on the court intending to mess up in front of their family and friends. What are you really accomplishing with your anger? Poor decisions and mental mistakes can be addressed in practice, but players should not be criticized for physical mistakes. Check your intent.

TEAM CHEMISTRY WORKSHEETS – PART I

Individual Worksheet

Each player completes this by themselves:

1. List a few situations where you are aware that you use your words against yourself.

2. As Dr. Phil would say, "How's that workin' for ya?" If it's not working for you, what process might work better?

Group Worksheet

Discuss each point and write the responses on a white board:

1. How might the acceptance of this "agreement" (speaking with impeccability) benefit our team?

2. Can we agree to adopt this agreement? Do you have reservations? If so, what pitfalls do we have to avoid and what worries you about it?

3. Would you like to re-phrase or state the agreement in another way?

4. List a few specific situations where we would need to be vigilant about this agreement?

Agreement 2
Don't take anything personally

- Nothing others do is because of you. What others say and do is a projection of their own reality, their own insecurity and their own ideas. When you are not vulnerable to the opinions and actions of others, you won't be the victim of needless anguish or torment.

- Nothing other people do is because of you – it is because of them. When we take something personally, we make the assumption that others know what we think and feel, which is usually impossible.

- Even when a situation seems so personal, even if others insult you directly, it has nothing to do with you. Their point of view comes from all the programming they received during their upbringing – it is all their feelings, beliefs and opinions. Taking things personally makes you easy prey; it can become toxic to you. If you take in all their emotional garbage, it becomes your garbage.

- When you feel offended, your reaction is to defend your beliefs and create conflicts. You may make something big out of something little because you have the need to be right and make everyone else wrong.

- As you make a habit of not taking anything personally, you won't need to place your trust in what others say about you, or what they do. You will only need to trust yourself to make responsible choices. When we are afraid (often about what others think), we often lash out. If you don't take anything personally, you can live without fear, you can love yourself, you can be happy.

TEAM CHEMISTRY WORKSHEETS – PART II

Individual Worksheet

Each player completes this by themselves:

1. List a few situations where you are aware that you took things personally.

2. How are you affected by taking things personally? How can you process what people say or do in a way that might work better for you?

Group Worksheet

Discuss each point and write the responses on a white board:

1. How might the acceptance of this "agreement" (not taking anything personally) benefit our team?

2. Can we agree to adopt this agreement? Do you have reservations? If so, what worries you about it?

3. Would you like to re-phrase or state the agreement in another way?

4. List a few specific situations where we would need to be vigilant about this agreement?

Agreement 3
Don't make assumptions

- Find the courage to ask questions and to express what you really want and need. Communicate with others as clearly as you can to avoid misunderstandings, sadness, frustrations and drama. If you don't understand, ask. With just this one agreement, you can completely transform your life.

- When we make assumptions we are asking for problems. We make an assumption, we misunderstand, we take it personally, and we end up creating a big drama for nothing. We even assume people don't like/love us, and then we blame and reject ourselves.

- In relationships we often make the assumption that our partners/friends know us so well that they know what we think, feel and need. When they fail to meet our needs, we sulk, get hurt, mad or afraid and sometimes even start fights.

- We also make assumptions about ourselves, creating a lot of inner conflict. If you think (make the assumption) you can do something and then you discover you aren't able to do it, you are often left questioning yourself rather than finding out how to do it.

- You shouldn't have to justify why you like/love someone or think that your affections will change them (another assumption). Real love is accepting other people the way they are without trying to change them. Similarly, others shouldn't try to change you.

TEAM CHEMISTRY WORKSHEETS – PART III

Individual Worksheet

Each player completes this by themselves:

1. List a few situations where you are aware that you have made assumptions.

2. How has it affected you or your relationships when you've made assumptions? What's the single most important thing you could do to keep from making assumptions?

Group Worksheet

Discuss each point and write the responses on a white board:

1. How might the acceptance of this "agreement" (don't make assumptions) benefit our team?

2. Can we agree to adopt this agreement? Do you have reservations? If so, what worries you about it?

3. Would you like to re-phrase or state the agreement in another way?

4. List a few specific situations where we would need to be vigilant about this agreement?

Agreement 4
Always do your best

- Your best is going to change from moment to moment. It will be different when you're healthy as opposed to sick or injured. Under any circumstance, doing your best will help you avoid self-judgment, self-abuse and regret.

- Doing your best is taking action because you love

it, not because you are expecting a reward. If you only take action when you expect a reward or you are playing for someone else's satisfaction, you won't enjoy the action – you won't do your best. Enjoy the problem solving, enjoy life. If you're having fun, you won't get bored and you won't have frustrations. (Or, at least, you'll have lots fewer.)

- When you do your best, you learn to accept yourself. But you have to be aware and learn from your mistakes. Learning from your mistakes means you practice, look honestly at the results, set new goals and keep practicing. Journaling can be a helpful way to note and increase your awareness.

- You do your best because you want to do it, not because you have to do it, not because you are trying to please some "judge," and not because you are trying to please other people. It's your choice. You can say "yes" or "no."

- By doing your best, the habits of misusing your words, taking things personally, and making assumptions will become weaker and less frequent with time. You don't need to judge yourself, feel guilty, or punish yourself if you can't keep these agreements. If you are doing your best, you'll feel good about yourself, and eventually you will master them.

TEAM CHEMISTRY WORKSHEETS – PART IV

Individual Worksheet

Each player completes this by themselves:

1. List a few situations where you are aware that you have not done your best.
2. How has it affected you when you feel you have not done your best? What's the single most important thing you could do to let yourself feel like you are doing your best?

Group Worksheet

Discuss each point and write the responses on a white board:

1. How might the acceptance of this "agreement" (always do your best) benefit our team?

2. Can we agree to adopt this agreement? Do you have reservations? If so, what worries you about it?

3. Would you like to re-phrase or state the agreement in another way?

4. List a few specific situations where we would need to be vigilant about this agreement?

Final Group Discussion

1. How do you want our team to define good team chemistry?

2. Make a list of interpersonal behaviors that will enhance our team chemistry.

3. How and when do you want to monitor our progress?

Final Thoughts

Don't underestimate the value of team chemistry. Too often, coaches get stuck in the rut of totally focusing on skills, techniques and strategy. If you ever catch yourself wondering why your team lacks energy, enthusiasm or resilience, it's time to shift your focus. Sit back and observe the players' behaviors and how they interact on the court and from the bench. Are they a "team" or 6 individuals on the court? Are some players in their own little world? Is there good productive communication on the court? Can you tell some players talk to themselves or get angry with themselves? Are players on the bench engaged or distracted? What are your team huddles like? Is everyone paying attention or are there side conversations? It's likely they will need your intervention to solve some of these problems. Help them create better chemistry by adopting and molding new beliefs and behaviors. And don't forget that your own interactions with the team must be consistent and coherent.

6 Keys to Developing Competitive Team Spirit

"Coming together is a beginning;
keeping together is progress;
working together is success."

-Henry Ford

Teaching players to be more competitive is a topic that comes up frequently in coaching clinics. Rest assured, competitive behaviors can be taught – just like any other skill. But there's a difference between training individuals to be more competitive and training a TEAM to be more competitive. With a team, you're dealing with the complexity of group behavior. Molding individuals into a like-minded group presents many challenges. Nonconformists can create all sorts of hurdles. But, if you can get everyone to invest in the process, I firmly believe creating a competitive team spirit can be a life-changing experience for athletes.

Step 1
Identifying defeating behaviors

It's important for you to lead a discussion where players identify behaviors that impede their team's competitive spirit. Start by having one player record the comments on a white board. You might have to give the players some ideas from the "25 defeating behaviors list" to get them started. Your main objective is to help your team understand how one individual's undesirable actions can negatively influence everybody. Eventually, you want your team to be aware and vigilant about eliminating these behaviors. Help them develop an ability to substitute competitive behaviors that are positive and productive for defeating behaviors.

25 Defeating Behaviors

1. Make multiple errors / poor judgment

2. Lots of excuses

3. Start and/or finish badly

4. Afraid / distrustful

5. No energy or minimal energy

6. Reactive and blaming communication

7. Whiplash / behind the play

8. Bitching / cliques

9. Cancel success (e.g. great kill, then serve out)

10. Trying to be perfect

11. Lack of intention – no plan / stupid mistakes

12. Quiet / withdrawn

13. Unassertive / unforced errors (especially under stress)

14. Attitudes: poor; inappropriate

15. Rather be right than succeed

16. Refuse opportunity to close out a match

17. Allow teammates to fail

18. Confused / lack of clarity / don't know the score

19. Check out / shut down / not present

20. Focused on unimportant factors

21. Lack of responsibility / late/ forget stuff

22. No change after time-outs or subs

23. Big swings in emotional intensity

24. Play without enthusiasm

25. Torn apart by adversity

Step 2
Delete old behaviors

Getting players to buy into a new pattern of behavior is critical. Players have to choose to be part of this process or they will never totally accept your leadership. Tapping into the frustration of losing can be a powerful motivator. Pitch it to them as a new model for enhancing competitive excellence. Put the players into small groups, and have them complete these steps:

- Have the team identify their most common defeating behaviors.

- Have them identify the cue or event that engages the behavior.

- Have them choose a positive, substitute behavior for each defeating behavior. (This should be a behavior that can be communicated to the entire team with 1-3 key words.)

Step 3
Install a new model

Once players have identified unproductive behaviors, they should begin to form a new, productive model that includes:

- Collectively agreeing on the new choice.

- "Flipping the switch" to change old behaviors.

- Frequently revisiting the agreements and evaluating their progress.

Example of how Steps 2 and 3 might unfold:

Players have identified a problem as "starting slow in matches."

Deleting that behavior

- Problem: Lack of intensity, intention and energy in warm-up, resulting in the team not being ready physically or mentally to start the match.

- Cue/event that engages the defeating behavior. It might be gathering slowly without energy and without intention for the pre-game meeting with the coach.

Installing a new model

- All players agree to be on time for the meeting, ready for warm-up and bring their "best self" to the warm-up. (Have them define their "best self.")

- Captains may have to be responsible for reminding others of their agreements.

- Do spot checks to see how everyone feels about agreements and what kind of effect the agreement is having on the old problem of starting slow in a match.

Step 4
Establish guidelines for team behavior

1. The coach is in charge. Players look to you for guidance.

2. Talk to your team about what kind of personality they want to have. For example:

    - What types of activities enhance group cohesion and readiness to play? One of my teams decided they should talk about the game and scouting report on the way to the gym rather than being in their own little world with headphones.

    - Do they want to display "togetherness." For example: Walking into the gym together, dressed alike, no headphones.

    - What kind of behaviors would show their "team personality?"

3. Define acceptable and unacceptable behavior – before, during and after matches.

4. How will we handle winning and losing after a match – with officials, opponents, teammates, media and even parents – after the match and at the next practice?

5. What does it mean to be a good loser or classy winner?

6. The time between points (dead-ball time) is critical. Talk about what a winning team looks like in dead-ball time. This must be practiced. If behaviors like negative self-talk and shutting out the coach or teammates are allowed, they will only become exaggerated in a match.

7. What comments are acceptable and unacceptable to a member of the media?

8. Winning and losing should not be linked with self-esteem.

9. What are the behaviors they have totally within their control? For example:

    - Knowing your responsibilities.

    - Giving your best effort.

    - Having a winning posture on the court.

    - Communicating in a positive way.

    - Figuring out how to be successful.

Step 5
Providing direction for competition

- Require players to run to the huddle. This keeps them from processing negative self-talk.

- Be intellectual about failures, not emotional. Getting mad isn't productive.

- During post-event analysis, let them be involved in evaluating their play.

- Tell your team to be aggressive – make aggressive mistakes.

- Demand animation, communication, running to position during play. Movement creates energy.

- Implement scripted substitutions as much as possible. Who does what, when and how.

- Control momentum. Don't lose more than a few points before reacting. Determine if the problem is emotional or strategic and change whatever is appropriate.

- Keep information simple. Players will usually only remember the last couple of things you say in a time-out.

- Never personally attack a player verbally.

- Keep the coaching comments as strategic as possible. Don't coach techniques.

- Prepare unscripted subs as much as possible. Let them know they might be going in at a specific position.

- Have "de-stressing" techniques to use when the team gets stressed. I've been known to make light of some situations. (e.g. "Now we have 'em right where we want 'em.") Tell a joke in the huddle, remind them of their strengths, or remind them of a time they pulled through in a similar situation.

Step 6
Main goals for the team

- Player initiated intensity. Necessary for being competitive.

- Increased communication. Call "Mine!" or "Ball!" Talk to who you are passing to, encourage your hitter, talk about what is happening and what might happen.

- Engage in figuring out how to be successful and how to get points.

- No judgment in defense – just go for it!

- Clarity in knowing assignments. Hit your assignments.

- Competitive posture at all times.

- Random but important thoughts.

- As soon as you quit trying, you become a victim. A competitor is never a victim.

- "Run your practice, not your mouth." –Russ Rose

- Be a problem-solver, not the problem.

- Learning how to tap into a competitive spirit is a skill that will help your players be more successful in all phases of their lives.

Managing Behaviors: Strategies to Help Players Monitor Themselves

"It is not our circumstances that create our discontent or contentment. It is us."

- Vivian Greene

One of the more difficult tasks in coaching is finding a way to help players understand how their behaviors can affect their athletic development. As a coach, you want to give them tools that will support them in enhancing and managing their physical, emotional and mental abilities.

An excellent way for players to make significant improvements is by using a journal to document their goals and their progress in these areas.

Help Players Become Self-Aware

Give your players some keys so they can understand what a "10" looks like.

In a journal or notebook they use during (or before) practice and after matches, they can rate themselves on a scale of 1 to 10 in each of the three categories below.

Coaches may initially do a "reality check" on the players' ratings of themselves. Use caution. Being too blunt can put an immediate damper on the entire process.

Physical

What a "10" looks like physically

- Sweating

- Alert – bright eyes

- Willingness postures

- Talkative, animated

- Working hard in warm-up

- On time – anticipation

What players who are not a "10" look like physically

- Slow-moving

- Crabby

- Quiet

5 Tools for Managing Physical Aspects of Self-Awareness

1. Metabolism - Have them remember when they played their best and how they felt. (Calm, excited, confident, nervous, etc.)

   - Pulse-arousal level - Controlling this can help with relaxation or energizing.

   - Breathing - Helps close or accelerate pulse/arousal.

   - Eyes - Making eye contact with teammates helps them connect and create bonds, taking focus off self and moving it to team.

2. Sleep, rest, food and workload - It's difficult to perform your best if these critical components aren't in balance. Have your players determine optimal levels for each.

3. Personal living space and locker-room space - Having neat and organized spaces helps calm the mind and gives a sense of well-being.

4. Social demands - Players must thoughtfully establish priorities for their time and be willing to limit some aspects, especially during the competitive season. Athletes often over-commit themselves, which can lead to fatigue and leave them prone to injuries.

5. Physical training and fitness - Committing to an offseason conditioning program allows for full, effective participation.

Emotional

What a "10" looks like emotionally

- Make eye contact

- Say things that are positive and productive

- Bring their best self

- Are receptive to comments from others

- Connect with teammates physically with high fives, touches on the shoulder, etc.

What players who are not a "10" look like emotionally

- They mumble

- They isolate themselves

- They swear

- They're not engaging

5 Tools for Managing Emotions

1. Attention to being "on task"

   - Discuss the upcoming match on the way to the match or before it. This begins the process of focusing on the game plan and strategies.

   - Ask the right questions during the match. Deal with the future, not past plays or events.

   - Focus on how to get the next point. Where can I hit? Who are the best blockers? Who are the weakest blockers? Talk about what you will do. Non-specific talk like, "Come on, let's go" is rarely helpful.

2. Don't use your words or thoughts against yourself - This totally undermines performance and distracts you from the task at hand.

3. Agreements set with yourself and teammates create your beliefs - Team meetings are helpful to discuss these important team aspects. Everyone needs to understand and buy into the beliefs/ visions.

   - Who you are as a team - A good blocking team? Strong passers? Good at focusing on tasks?

- What you believe - For example, we are resilient, trustworthy, competitive, etc.

- What you feel - Faith in teammates, warrior-like, etc.

- How you behave/respond - How does the team enter the gym? How do you respond to coaching, poor officiating, adversity, victory, defeat?

4. Have the courage to break agreements that are self-defeating

   - Frustration causes players to lose their focus on the team or on their roles. It inhibits growth. Have each player journal about their frustrations and how they will recognize them and then let them go.

   - Other fear-based agreements - anger, fear, choking, withdrawing, divisive gossip, etc.

   - Extend conversation - How can team members create good morale on and off the court? What is good conversation and what is poor conversation?

Mental

What a "10" looks like mentally:

- Focus on the opponent

- Anticipate – know what will happen next

- Have clarity in the moment

- Create strategies to stay ahead

- Have a clear sense of the importance of actions

- Alert teammates to advantages they see

What players who are not a "10" look like mentally:

- Focus on themselves

- Lose track of the score

- Are unaware of opponents

3 Tools for Managing Mental Aspects of Self-awareness

1. Clearing the emotional body/awareness

    - Know when emotions are getting in your way and have a plan to remedy each situation - over-arousal, anger, fear, frustration.

- Don't get stuck - Have a definite refocus plan. Writing it down helps players remember what to do.

- Don't judge yourself - It's self-defeating.

- Be a problem-solver, not a problem - Recognize when you can help yourself and/ or the team.

2. Competitive commitments – your mental mindset

- Give your best effort - It's all right to expect that this effort will be different on different days. You're not a robot!

- Make a play - Discuss examples of the best play for specific situations – like a bad pass or a bad set or a great set in front of a big blocker – and then practice these situations.

3. Confidence that skills can get you what you want

- How many reps does it take for a shift?

- Can you believe unconditionally? - If not, why not? And how can you change this?

Final Thoughts

Get players to ask the right questions; this is critically important.

- If you ask what you did wrong, you will probably get an answer that's not helpful. For example, "Why do I keep getting aced?" (I'm slow, bad platform.)

- Instead, ask how to get better. This will help you figure out ways to improve. For example, "How can I pass more consistently?" (I can read the server, move, get my platform ready early.)

Dealing with the Doldrums

Consistent success in volleyball often depends on the coach's ability to keep players engaged throughout the season. Here are some strategies that will help.

The midpoint of your season has just passed, and it never fails. Your team hits the "doldrums." Unfortunately, it usually happens right in line with the time when results in critical games can make or break your season.

To define terms, the doldrums as they relate to your team are marked by any or all of these issues:

- Players display boredom, low energy or no energy.

- Players are consumed by academic priorities.

- Players are dealing with physical fatigue and injuries.

- Lack of team success leads to low team and/or individual morale and mental fatigue.

- Stress creates interpersonal strain between team members and/or coaches.

The accumulation of these distractions can result in waning enthusiasm. As their coach, it's important that you try to solve or at least mitigate these issues. Without intervention of some type, goals for the season may not be achieved.

With that in mind, I'd like to share some actions that have been helpful to me through the years.

Give Them Time Off

I shake my head in disbelief at coaches who decide that all of the issues listed above can be cured by tougher practices. I can't stress enough that this is exactly opposite of what research tells us. Giving the players a day or two off practice can refresh them, both physically and mentally. And let's face it, how much are you really going to accomplish in practice if they're mentally checked out and physically drained?

Two Personal Days

This is a policy I established at the beginning of each season. Each player got two personal days. By notifying me no later than noon, they could take the day off to do whatever they need – rest, study, enjoy a mental break, whatever. The only limitations were that they could not use a personal day for the day before a match because we would be putting in the game plan and discussing the scouting report. (Injuries and illness, as confirmed by our athletic trainer, should not require taking a personal day.)

This policy created 3 important benefits. First, there was no judgment required from me as to the importance of their request. Second, it gave the players a sense of control over their lives. And third, it ended any begging for special consideration to miss practice, often accompanied by their most inventive reasons.

Some of my players used both days every year, others rarely used them. I found that players mostly took personal days in the second half of the season – just as the stress began to pile up. I once had an assistant coach who asked to take a personal day. I had to explain that this policy was only for the players, not the coaching staff. Coaches have their share of bad days too, but hopefully we have the maturity to put aside whatever issues come up and focus on what's best for our team.

Team Check-in Before Practice

Before warm-up, we would always sit on the floor in a circle, coaches included. Each person had between 30-45 seconds to share something important or special about their day. Routinely, players would talk about tests or homework, good news they had, sometimes bad news. Sometimes they were sick or tired, sometimes they were totally fired up. They could share anything they wanted, but I cautioned them about over-sharing and maintaining good personal boundaries. They always had to end with, "And I'm ready for practice," or, "But (despite all this), I'm ready for practice." If they didn't have anything to share, they could just say, "Pass … and, "I'm ready for practice." On rare occasions, I would have to lightheartedly tell someone to "wrap it up." Players were usually respectful about not taking more than their allotted time.

Make sure players understand that this is NOT a therapy session; they shouldn't expect advice or comments. Coaches and team members are there to hear and acknowledge their check-in without comment. (An occasional chuckle is OK.)

Benefits of a Check-in

This entire process only takes 10-12 minutes, and it's well worth the time because it reaps many positives, including:

- Daily insight into your players' lives. How are they feeling? What stressors are affecting them? If they report that they've had a horrible day or a major disappointment, you might be inclined to cut them some slack in practice, give them a pat on the back or find time to talk to them one-on-one.

- An opportunity for every player to have a few moments to be in the spotlight and have everyone's attention. You'll find that shy players eventually come out of their shells and communicate with the team and coaches. It also reveals a lot about each person's basic personality.

- A chance for you to engage with your players, which affirms you as part of the team. It also humanizes you as someone who has good and bad days too.

- It brings the entire team together at the beginning of practice with everyone agreeing that they're ready to practice.

In my experience, most everyone uses good judgment about personal boundaries. The sharing was appropriate, without getting too personal or revealing. If it ever crossed the line, I would say something privately to the player or coach.

I used the check-in for many years and found it to be really helpful. In fact, it became one of the highlights of practice. At many of our alumni games, players arrived and asked if they could have a check-in before they started their warm-up.

Individually Written "Why I Appreciate You" Notes

Do you know anyone who doesn't like to get positive feedback? I sure don't. During the doldrums, I wrote individual notes to each player and left them in their lockers. It takes a little time, but I guarantee it will act as a pick-me-up. Of course, you have to be sincere and believable. Find something you admire about them, what makes them a good teammate, how you appreciate things they do for the team. Comment on their strengths or what they have overcome to be a good player.

Surprise Movie Day

Watching game film, whether it's your own team or the opponents, can be tedious. Rarely do players enjoy it. So surprise them one day by popping in a fun movie or comedy. Get some popcorn and soft drinks or juice and have a little party. Of course, you won't want this to take the place of your normal pre-match prep for an opponent. But it might be the perfect remedy for overcoming a particularly stinging loss. Who wants to be reminded of a terrible performance in the midst of the doldrums?

Final Thoughts

Creating a team culture that is less prone to the doldrums goes beyond the drills you run and the skills you teach. It's about investing in your players and their lives on a deeper level, caring what their days are like before they get to the gym and after they leave. Often, the effort you make to show that you're concerned with more than just how well they pass, set and hit will pay big dividends when it comes time to take the court.

Defeating Distractions:
Strategies to Help Players Stay Focused

"To achieve greatness, you must be willing to surrender ambition."
- Carol Osborn, Ph.D.

For a coach, there's nothing more frustrating than looking out on the court at a critical time in a match and seeing one or more players laughing with someone in the crowd or sulking about a previous play. Unfocused players are responsible for a fair share of a coach's gray hair!

But, as most coaches quickly figure out, you can't just command them to focus. It's imperative to teach them about how to deal with the inevitable distractions they will face.

If athletes can learn to recognize and overcome distractions, they'll be better individual competitors and, in turn, better team members. Using a journal to work through this process can be an effective tool for players.

Step 1
What is a distraction?

In a team meeting, ideally during the offseason or preseason, lead a discussion asking team members to give examples of distracting events, behaviors, or actions. Write them on a white board. They should all generally fall into these categories:

- **Something that diverts or draws your attention away from the tasks at hand.** At a rival's gym with a loud crowd, several fans are taunting you by saying unflattering things as you rotate to the front row to hit.

- **Thoughts that interrupt or disrupt your thinking.** As you walk back to serve, you see your parents walk into the gym and recall the big argument you had with them the last time you saw them. Are they still mad? Should you apologize?

- **Interruptions to your focus.** In a tight game, you are a primary passer getting ready to receive the serve and the coach calls a time-out. In the huddle, the coach gives instructions about the opposing blockers and talks to the setter about options for sets but says nothing about what to expect from the server and doesn't offer any encouragement about passing. You leave the huddle thinking about the coach.

- **Irritations, actions, talking or behavior that affect those around you.** One of your teammates has a tendency to talk negatively and pout when not playing well. Despite team discussion about curtailing this type of behavior, it continues to cause problems.

Step 2
Recognizing distractions for yourself.

Ask players to spend time alone identifying events, actions, people or behaviors that are distracting to them and may cause them to lose focus. They should be able to identify several different situations. In great detail, they should answer these important questions:

- How, when and where do you become distracted?

- What behaviors do you display when you are distracted?

Step 3
My most outstanding distraction.

In a quiet environment, have players write down a vivid, detailed description of the distraction that is most common and/or most disruptive to them. When does it happen? Who is there? Where does it happen? How does it affect them?

Step 4

Make a detailed "refocus plan" for how you will overcome distractions when you become aware of them.

- Individually, each player outlines a simple plan to help regain focus. The plan could be the same for every distraction or different for each one. The important thing is for the player to be able to implement the plan quickly. Here are some examples:

  - Snap a rubber band on your wrist. Take a deep breath. Focus on your job for the next play.

  - Take 2 deep breaths and make eye contact with a teammate. Tell your teammates what you will be responsible for on the next play.

  - Stand up straight with shoulders back, breathe deeply, positively engage a teammate.

Step 5

Recognizing how you may distract the team.

Players need to acknowledge that they may have behaviors that can be a distraction to their team. Again, they will spend time alone to consider situations or actions from the past that may have been distracting to the team in general or to specific individuals. If players have trouble identifying any situations like this, the coach may help by asking questions like:

- How, when and where do you become a distraction to your team?

- What behaviors do you display when you distract the team?

Step 6
Make a detailed plan to overcome being a distraction to the team.

This step can be difficult, especially if players are unaware of their behavior. For the unaware player, suggest that they solicit information from a good friend, team captain or, less ideally, a coach. Ask them to tell you about any distracting behaviors they have seen you exhibit. You may also ask them to tell you when these behaviors actually happen. Eventually, each player must take accountability of their actions without relying on teammates. This plan should encompass accepting personal responsibility and being committed to a rapid change of behavior.

Step 7
Group and team discussion.
(Allow 30-40 minutes)

After completing steps 2-6 individually, players will come together as a team. The coach can randomly assign players to groups of 3 or 4. In the small groups, players will:

- Share personal insights about their own tendencies for distraction. (Some players may be uncomfortable sharing specific information. If that's an issue, encourage them to share generalizations.)

- Share specific "refocus plans" for dealing with distractions.

- Share thoughts about how they personally plan to become aware and then overcome being a distraction to the team.

Step 8

Share group discussion highlights with the team.
(Allow 30-40 minutes)

The coach should make sure that every group and each individual participates in some way. Ask the players to wrap up the session with some common themes; write them on a white board.

Final Thoughts

Productive habits are formed through persistent attention. Before each team practice, give players a few minutes to jot down some goals related to recognizing distractions and then using their refocus plans.

After matches, have players evaluate the success of recognizing when they were distracted and how effectively they used their refocus plans.

The coach also needs to discuss this important aspect of player development during short, regularly scheduled individual meetings.

Bitching:
The Greatest Threat to Athletic Progress

"When we are no longer able to change a situation, we are challenged to change ourselves."
-Viktor E. Frankl

The title of this article probably made you smile, but as you consider it a bit more, you might think about what a big problem bitching can be for coaches and athletes. Earlier you read an article titled "10 Steps to Improving a Player's Personal Motivation" that discussed helping individuals come to the realization that they control their own lives. Here, I'd like to offer some insight into how bitching just might be the biggest obstacle to personal achievement and improved performance. Taking personal responsibility for your situation – and your response to each situation – can create dramatic transformations. Let's start with a five-point overview of the anatomy and psychology of bitching – who we bitch with, why we bitch and what we bitch about.

1. **Friends who bitch together**
   Friends tend to bitch about similar things. In sports, friends bitch about their teammates, their coaches, their opponents, daily schedules and the

expectations of their coach. They can often be heard saying things like, "I can't believe we have to do this!" Coaches often bitch about players, officials, athletic directors – you get the idea. If you think about it, we often associate ourselves with people who have similar perspectives.

2. **Getting others to bitch with you**

If players can get others to commiserate with them by bitching, they often feel justified in their discontent. Complaining always seems to absolve a person of their disgruntlement and personal responsibility. By sharing their unhappiness and getting a cohort to agree, it helps you feel justified. You might hear, "I knew I wasn't the only one who thought this was terrible!" And don't forget the coaching side of it. Ever had a discussion with another coach and said, "I knew I wasn't the only one who had a problem with this kid"? When coaches do this, they're trying to absolve themselves of their responsibility to unravel issues with a player. But putting all the blame on the player rarely accomplishes anything.

3. **Bitching is the best defense**

The best defense is a good offense. What bitching implies is, "It's not my fault or responsibility – it's the fault of the coaches, the officials, trainers or my teammates." By bitching they also might finagle themselves out of doing what they really need to do but are resisting.

4. Bitching gives away your power to succeed

Athletes and coaches rarely realize how the act of bitching takes away their personal power. One issue I discussed earlier in this book is the importance of accepting personal responsibility. It's a critical aspect of personal growth. We need to have a willingness to accept failures as part of the learning or growth process. Think about a toddler beginning to walk. They repeatedly fall down. Do they respond by slapping the floor, swearing and giving up? No. They shrug it off, get up and try again. There's no judgment about what a useless human being they are or about how walking is way too hard. Bitching is a learned behavior and defense mechanism that blocks the innate process of learning.

5. Bitching provides a great excuse

Bitching not only gives people emotional cover from having to deal with failure, it provides a distraction in the form of an excuse. People get mad or frustrated and refuse to do any problem-solving or introspection; that's a lot more difficult. I would always tell players that everyone has hurdles to overcome – either emotional, mental or physical. Individuals who have become accomplished in their field – like great athletes, award-winning writers or business leaders – have a willingness to engage their personal hurdles. They become proficient and obsessed with successfully overcoming their obstacles. They choose to become an actor, not a victim. And they choose to take personal accountability for their situation.

The solution

This my golden rule of coaching: awareness leads to change. Unless players become aware of unproductive behaviors, there's little hope the behavior will change. Bitching and denial prevent change. Here are my suggestions for eliminating this behavior from the team environment. Coaches should participate, too. Joining in will humanize you to the team.

- Assign each player to spend some time individually journaling about their tendencies to bitch – with whom, about whom, when, where? What does this bitching do for you? Are they really enjoying playing? Do they want to continue? What do they get out of playing and being a member of the team? Remind them they are in charge of their life.

- Does this bitching help or inhibit your progress as an athlete and in becoming a valuable member of the team? Give some examples.

- With one or two close friends (who know you well and will be honest with you), check to see if your personal reflections are consistent with how they view your behaviors.

- In a team meeting, share some of your personal observations about yourself. CAUTION FOR COACHES ... keep this light. It can end up being a funny and productive experience if it doesn't get too serious. Coaches should share some personal reflections. For example, one time I shared how I got irritated when they had trouble with a drill in practice and I bitched up a storm about them after practice. Then I told them that I finally realized that it wasn't their performance in the drill that made me mad. Rather, it was the crappy drill I had designed! They got a real charge out of that admission. It opened the door for them to be more forthcoming. It's good to let them know that it's normal for them to bitch about you, their coach.

- Give them a few minutes to consider what they might be accomplishing with bitching. Have them include when, where and with whom it usually happens. Ask if this helps them become better players. If not, what changes will they try to make? One player volunteered to make "No Bitching Zone" stickers for their lockers.

- Finally, have them do some problem-solving as a group about things they can do for themselves and each other to reduce the unproductive behavior of bitching.

Trust Building Strategies to Promote Team Bonding

"The best and most beautiful things in the world cannot be seen or even touched. They must be felt with the heart."
- Helen Keller

A team is like a living organism. The atmosphere can change instantly, morphing into positive, negative or sluggish energy. The many moving pieces continually create situations where relationships between players and coaches are tested. Interdependence is vital to working effectively together. Trust is the bond that can successfully connect individuals. This quality allows the collective group to be more resilient and to conquer the inevitable adversity that comes with each season. In order to build trust, it's important to understand the many components of trust that are in play within a team.

Here's a quick overview:

Interpersonal Trust

We trust those who do what they say they will do. It's kind of a no brainer. It's impossible to trust someone who routinely fails to do what they promised to do and fails to give a rational explanation. Stuff happens, but it can't happen all the time!

Organizational Trust

We trust another person who we're in a relationship with – either personally or professionally – if we believe they will act for the betterment of our relationship or for the betterment of the team vs. the betterment of themselves.

Mistrust

This is a simple concept: a person who continually betrays your trust will never be trusted. Often, this results in impenetrable walls going up as protection.

Cooperation

When people cooperate, it's (almost) always a path to the greatest benefit for the individual, the team and the organization as a whole. Efforts to use collaboration, teamwork and mutual support effectively build trust.

Trust is Fragile

It takes only one person to violate trust. It takes everyone to maintain it. Every team member must be dedicated to maintaining the sacred bonds of trust.

To regain trust we must:

- Talk about what happened.

- Understand why our behavior was seen as a violation of trust.

- Be genuinely sorry. It's important for trust-violators to make it clear that they didn't intend for the violation to occur.

- Earn trust back by:

    1. Being trustworthy over a long period of time.

    2. Being trustworthy when the stakes are higher.

Small Group Activity

Divide the team into small groups of 3 to 4 players. Be sure to include different age levels in each group. Ask them to give at least one specific example of a trust issue in each of the above categories. These should be related to a team situation. For example, in the organizational trust area, the group might come up with an example of when a player gave up their desire to be a captain or another leadership position when it became clear they were not the choice of the team. Allow at least 20 minutes for this small group activity.

Sharing Small Group Examples

Have each group share their example in one area so the entire team covers one aspect before moving on to the next area of trust.

Team Discussion

In a group where everyone participates, have the team discuss these specific issues:

- What aspects of trust do you think will be the biggest challenge?

- What are some simple things we can do as individuals to build trust?

- What are some simple things we can do as a team to build trust?

- How will building trust help our team?

- What can the coaches do to help build trust? You may have to pry this out of them, but before you try, offer your own thoughts about what you can do yourself.

Direction from the Coach

Remember, the role of the coach is critical in this process. In case you haven't thought about it, make sure you spend some time considering your past actions. It's likely there have been instances where your coaching decisions or techniques failed to enhance trust with the players and team. Fess up and tell the team that you will try to do better. (See "regaining trust" above.) Confession is good for the soul and an excellent way to repair trust with your team.

The Celebration Phenomenon: Changing the Energy Level of Your Team

"If the only tool you have is a hammer, you tend to see every problem as a nail."
– Abraham Maslow

We've all been there. You're sitting on the bench watching your team swirl down the drain. Players have their heads down and are muttering to themselves with no connection to each other and no acceptable level of effort. If the match is to be salvaged, something needs to change quickly.

We all know what an engaged team looks like – good communication, high fives, smiles, eye contact, quick huddles at mid-court after each point, laughs (at appropriate times) and plenty of movement. In simple terms, these behaviors describe a team playing with positive energy. Many years ago, I wondered if there was anything a coach could do to encourage this energy at times when it's non-existent. It occurred to me that being able to almost instantly create a celebratory mood on the court might be the answer.

How do you describe "playing well"?

Before practice one day, we had a short team discussion. I asked my players what it looks like and feels like when they're playing well. I wrote their responses on a board under either "looks like" or "feels like." Here are the characteristics they settled on:

Looks like:

- We look happy.

- We are talkative.

- We are having a good time.

- We shake off mistakes.

- Everyone on the court is "together" or supporting each other.

- No ball drops without a good effort to keep it up.

Feels like:

- We are connected and constantly engage each other.

- We are confident.

- We play hard and give great effort all the time.

- We are positive and look forward, not backward.

Finally, I asked them if they could come up with just one word to describe what it looks like and feels like to be part of these behaviors. With some hints and a little prodding from me, they settled on "celebration." They all agreed it felt like being part of a celebration, sort of like being at a party. Coaching hint: I learned long ago that sometimes you have to trick your team into agreeing or believing what might be best for them.

Creating the Celebration and Changing the Energy

Just like with any other technique or strategy, practice is an important component. I should note that I presented this "celebration" concept as something we could use as a strategy to increase our energy level on the court when it seemed necessary. It would give them a plan for something we didn't currently have in our play book.

Once everyone agreed to the concept, we talked about winning and losing. It's important for players to understand that they can only control their own behavior. Although their behavior is important, it will not guarantee winning. The outcome is often beyond our control. It was also important for everyone to commit to using this strategy and technique by fully participating in creating the atmosphere. One non-participant can ruin the entire vibe.

Practicing Celebration

Set your team up on the court in a scrimmage situation with 2 full teams. Put the ball in play with a serve and play it out. The cue to begin the celebration on BOTH sides of the net occurs as soon as the ball is dead. For example, on a kill, a hitting error, an illegal set, a net foul, etc. This is important: Both sides must celebrate, even the team that loses the rally. When a team makes numerous mistakes, behaviors like drooping heads and mumbling begin, sapping the energy and life from the team. This is exactly the behavior you want to disrupt and why teams have to celebrate even after losing a point. The players developed their own preferences for celebrating as soon as they lost their inhibitions. We even named one player the "celebration captain," someone who was uninhibited and would usually be on the court. The point was to "fake it until they could make it." During a match, I could cue the celebration without a time-out by raising my index finger and twirling it around. I'm telling you, it was magical. Not only did the opposing team stare dumbfounded at what we were doing, especially when we lost the point, but our team found it to be very effective in helping them get out of their funk and into a more positive, productive place. You may only have to celebrate for a part of a game to get the effect. The point is to have a technique the team can use to change the energy level and focus.

Testimony to the Effectiveness of Celebration

We were playing one of the top teams in our conference. We had slipped into a lethargic routine and were quiet, joyless and disconnected. I called a time-out and told the players we had to start full-out celebration. As the huddles broke, they heard the opposing coach yell, "Hurry up and win before they start all the celebrating stuff!" My players turned around and smiled at me. We made an incredible energy shift and won the match. And that happened time and again during the season. The funniest thing is, I heard from several parents that the team was so fun to watch because we looked like we were having fun. And on those days when practice was dragging, we would turn to celebration, which immediately picked up the pace.

Tales from the Bench and the Gym

Most coaches are born storytellers. I love getting together with coaches and former players and reliving our shared experiences or hearing their stories. Invariably, some stories are permanently seared into your memory bank. Here are a few of mine.

Modern Technology

I never wanted to admit that I might be behind the curve in the technology trends for college athletes, but I was. Texting, Facebook, Instagram, Snapchat – none of them were in my wheelhouse. I did understand that college athletes were obsessed with their cell phones. I just didn't understand how obsessed.

One evening, during a hotly contested match, I jumped up from the bench and called one of our freshmen to substitute in. As I yelled her name, I saw that she was focused on her phone, seemingly texting someone. She was so engaged, she didn't even hear me. The entire bench looked at her with a sense of dread. I walked over and confiscated her phone, much to her shock. I told her I would return it after the match. She never played. As we loaded onto the bus after the match, I called her over and returned her cell phone but told her to bring it to practice the next afternoon. She looked startled and confused. I said I would explain the next day. When she arrived at practice, I told her that, in light of her enthusiasm for texting, I wanted her to find a comfy place to sit and watch practice while texting me EVERYTHING we did. She was incredulous, but I told her she had better get settled because we were about to begin. Never again did we have a problem with players using cell phones at inappropriate times.

Undisclosed Health Issues

I was with my University of Minnesota team at Iowa, shortly after they opened their new arena. I had been recruiting and was just joining the team in time for warm-up. When I entered the arena, I saw our team already on the court, but our starting freshman outside hitter was sitting on the bench crying.

I calmly walked over and asked what the matter was and why she wasn't warming up.

"I can't see," she said. "The lights are too bright!"

"What do you mean you can't see?" I asked.

"My cataracts – the lights are too bright and I can't see when I look up."

I was aghast. "Cataracts?!"

"Yeah," she responded in sobs. "I've had them since I was young."

I responded that it was too bad she had never mentioned this fact before. I asked her to try to go hit a ball from her outside hitter position. She did, and she missed the whole ball. I asked if she had sunglasses. She said she did but that they were at home. No one on our team had sunglasses.

After the match, I talked to her and said we had to get this figured out because she couldn't sit on the bench when the lights were bright. My mind was racing through a mental inventory of other Big Ten schools with bright lights. She promised she would go to the eye doctor when she got home and get something that would allow her to see. It was near the end of the season, so the cataract problem didn't come up again until the off-season. When we did talk about it, the player told me she had some goggles and she thought they would work. She never brought them to practice, despite my almost daily reminders. Finally, it was her sophomore year and it started with me saying, "Bring your goggles to practice." She never did but kept telling me she was wearing them around the dorm and they were good.

A match at Iowa was one of our first that season. I was recruiting again and meeting the team at the arena. I managed to get to the arena early as I was worried about the goggles. I quickly scanned the arena and focused in on our cataract kid. She was wearing metallic swim goggles! Did I mention she is 6 feet tall and has bright red "Little Orphan Annie" style hair? On her first warm-up hit, she missed the whole ball – again. I approached her and she said, "Gee, these goggles are fogging up." I thought to myself, "No s---, Sherlock!" As Iowa began to warm up, our trainer tried to cut off the foam rubber from around the goggles. The team was totally unfocused, and I was trying to be calm. The trainer managed to get the foam rubber cut off, and she tried the goggles again. This time, she didn't totally miss the ball, but she shanked it 30 feet wide of the court into the stands. Then she explained, "My vision is kind of distorted." I suggested that it was probably because they were supposed to be used under water, not on the court. She started crying again.

The final insult of the night came during the match. A huge crowd had gathered in the arena for the men's basketball team's first practice. We were playing horribly. I stood, called a time-out, and began to move toward the sideline – about 15 feet. Unbeknownst to me, my purse had become entangled in the leg of my folding chair and my foot was entangled in my purse strap. I was stuck, so I basically hopped on one foot, dragging the chair out to the huddle as my players tried to hide their amusement and the crowd roared with laughter. The players on our bench weren't even trying to hide their hilarity. By the time I got near the sideline, the time-out was almost over. My only hope was that this change in focus would result in improved play. It did not.

In case you are wondering, that outside hitter transferred the next year.

Coaching Strategy vs. Officials

My first full-time coaching job was at the University of Alabama. I was hired as the head volleyball and head basketball coach in the brand new women's athletic program. That first year, I arrived on campus after school had already started and we had matches coming up in 10 days. The only way to field a team was through open tryouts. After our first few practices, I found myself hoping the administration would give me a couple of years before judging my coaching skills. We were a rag-tag bunch with very little experience, but the players were all bright-eyed and wanted to learn.

My first problem was setting. I identified two players who I thought had leadership ability and decided we would train both to set. One was Vivian Langley, a freshman who eventually became a long-time assistant coach and treasured friend. I thought it would be cool to teach her the soft set, which was all the rage in Minnesota. She got pretty good at it. But, unfortunately, no one in Alabama, especially the officials, had ever seen a soft set. Our other setter had "straight, stone fingers" and although it sounded terrible when she contacted the ball, it was a legal set and she was pretty accurate.

We headed to Mississippi for our first tournament with everyone excited and eager to show off their skills. In our first match, the officials called Vivian for a throw every time she touched the ball. I tried to talk to them between games, but it became clear that they just considered me a "know-it-all Yankee," maybe even a damn Yankee. So our other setter went in, and they also called it every time she touched the ball because they were calling by the sound of the contact.

My solution? I called a time-out and told the team that every time the setter set the ball, they had to yell "SET" as loud as they could. The officials never called another illegal contact because they couldn't hear the sound. As a matter of fact, they told me after the match that she really cleaned up her sets after she got called a few times. It was supposed to be a compliment.

Understanding all the Rules of the Game

We were playing at Iowa, and I was coaching against one of the greats of our game, Ruth Nelson, a Hall of Famer and a good friend. The match was tight, back and forth. Three times during the match Ruth's great, senior setter was called for overlapping.

After the match, Ruth and I were talking, and I said, "What was the deal with your setter getting called for overlapping?"

"You are absolutely not going to believe this," she replied. She said she went to her setter after the match and asked the same question.

Her setter's response: "Maybe you could go over that overlapping rule with me again."

Out of Sight, Out of Mind

Back in the mid 1970s, when I was coaching at Alabama, the only time we could get facilities to do weight lifting and conditioning was at 6 a.m. It was brutal, but there was no other choice – women did not get any priority with facilities. As we started preseason practice, the players had a phone tree to make sure everyone got up in time to be at the track and weight room at 6. One of my players, Dorothy Franco-Reed, missed one morning and I didn't see her until practice that afternoon. For the good of team discipline, I felt I had to enforce dedication to be at morning workouts. So, when she arrived at practice, I told her that she needed to make up the time she'd missed that morning. I instructed her to go outside and run around Foster Auditorium (our practice facility) until I came out to tell her to stop. It was August in Alabama and about 90-plus degrees and 90-plus percent humidity. In other words, miserable.

Well, I totally forgot about her. About an hour after I instructed her to run around the building, she came dragging into the gym. I saw her coming in and thought, "Oh, geez!" She staggered up to me and said, "Is my time up?" I quickly decided I couldn't let on that I had forgotten about her, looked at my watch and said, "Nope, 5 more minutes!" You should have seen the looks of horror on the faces of her teammates.

Neither Dorothy nor anyone else was ever late again for morning workouts that year. That event has become legend for those players at Alabama. I should mention that Dorothy, thankfully, also became one of my long-time assistant coaches and remains a very close friend.

It seems appropriate here to discuss physical punishment, just like what I used in this situation. I was guilty of mimicking methods used by coaches I grew up watching. I can't, in good conscience, criticize the actions of other coaches, but I can say that I began to think about the human aspects of coaching and how I wanted to relate to players. What exactly was I accomplishing with physical punishment? My answer was, nothing very productive. And I was possibly putting players in dangerous situations. Coaches may get some temporary respect for their toughness, but when players look back on their careers, it's likely they will feel less kindly about punishment they experienced at your hands. As I grew more experienced (and braver), I often spoke publicly about the negative impact of physical punishment. In my opinion, it's dangerous, counterintuitive and has no place in coaching at any level.

Players who Challenge You

In 1976, my third year at Alabama, we won our regional tournament and qualified for the AIAW National Championship in Austin, Texas. Needless to say, we were thrilled! Our team was very talented, but we had some unique individuals playing for us. One was a 6-3 freshman, Louise – a beautiful young woman who could have been a model. She had played on the national team when she was 16 years old but decided the highly structured environment was not for her. To put it graciously, she was a free spirit. But she was also the key link in bringing our team to an elite level.

During the season, it became clear that Louise had a nontraditional lifestyle and many wild boyfriends. But the other players loved her and often covered for her. There were many times when we were leaving town for a tournament where we had to drive the van by Louise's house and pick her up. Most times, she was sleeping on the front porch with her uniform in a paper bag. What can I say? It was a different time and place.

My understanding of Louise increased exponentially early in her freshman year. We went to Princeton for a tournament, and Louise's family was there as she was from Maryland. After the Friday games, Louise's mom came up and introduced herself. She was young, vivacious and energetic. She asked if Louise could go with her that night to eat and hang out. I said, "Sure." Then she said, "Yeah, after dinner I thought we could hit some Frat parties!" She was serious! You could have knocked me over with a feather. I told her that Louise should be back to the hotel by 10 p.m., and she looked at me like I had two heads and no sense of adventure. But that interchange gave me some special insight into Louise.

The day we were leaving Tuscaloosa for Austin on a 7:30 a.m. flight, I have to say I was worried about Louise. Everyone was at the gym on time, except for Louise. We waited and waited, and finally I sent the team to the airport. I headed over to Louise's house. She was not sleeping on the porch; she was nowhere to be found. Exasperated, I left for the airport and made it just in time to board the plane. As we were sitting in our seats, I glanced out the window and saw Louise running toward the plane with her paper bag in hand and the gate agent in hot pursuit. She did a scissor jump over the fence and ran up the stairway right before they rolled it away. They let her board after a little kerfuffle, and we were off to Austin!

Facing the Legends

Once we were at the 24-team AIAW Championship, we got our schedule for pool play. Unfortunately, we drew the University of Houston for our first match. Ruth Nelson, Hall of Fame Coach, was coaching Houston, with a star-studded cast of players. My team, in their first-ever National Championship, was about to face

Flo Hyman and Rita Crocket – two of the greatest players in USA Volleyball history. My players' knees were shaking during warmups. At my first time-out, after 5 points, I suggested that all the back-row players put their hands up over their heads and in front of their faces when Houston got ready to hit. I told the front-row players to put their hands, forearms and elbows over their head like a table top … and to not even block when Rita and Flo were hitting. They were traumatized before the first game was over.

Our second match was against UCLA, led by Hall of Famer Terry Condon and their All-American cast. It was a long day! But the moral to the story is, you have to experience playing against the best before you can compete with the best. We finished 9th in the nation the next year.

Recovering from a Stupid Team Policy

In my early years at Alabama, I determined that we should have "goal weights" for players and they had to maintain their weight, within two pounds of their goal, throughout the season. Shortly after I set this policy, I had major regrets – for many reasons. Sadly, these were the days when many coaches thought it was a good idea to set this type of policy. I must say, with what we all now know about how women struggle with body image, I'm ashamed that this was a policy I thought was good. The fact that I was a young coach was not a good excuse.

As the season wore on, players were getting closer and closer to missing the cut for their goal weight. We weighed in every Thursday, and starting on Tuesday I would see some of the players running in rubber suits around campus. I knew I had made a big mistake with this policy, but I was too proud to abandon it. Many of our players were barely making the cut. Toward the end of the season, we were getting ready to play our arch rival, Auburn. It was a big match and I thought it was likely that our starting setter might miss her goal weight. So, the night before weigh in, after all the players had cleared out of the locker room, I went in and broke our scale! What else could I do?

The next day after practice, I told the players to go with our assistant coach and weigh in. A few minutes later, our setter came out of the locker room and said,

"Coach, the scale is broken!"

"Oh don't give me that excuse," I said. "Get in there and weigh in."

"No, really," she said, **"it's broken."**

I walked into the locker room and looked at the scale and said, "OK, which one of you broke the scale? Come on, fess up!"

They all denied doing it. I finally said, "Well, I guess

you all lucked out! I don't know how long it's going to take to get this thing fixed!"

Then I stormed out of the locker room. I imagine they all wondered which player broke the scale, but I'm sure they were happy as clams. We beat Auburn and never had another weigh in.

All these years later, I finally told many of them that I was the one who broke the scale. None of them ever thought it was me.

Strange but Effective Strategies

In 1989, I was honored to be selected to coach the North Team in the USA Olympic Festival. The Festival has since ceased to exist, but back then it was a huge event for many sports. Collegiate players participated in national tryouts, competing for positions on North, South, East or West teams. Everyone gathered for 5 days of team practices and then pool play competition against the other teams. It ended with playoffs and gold, silver and bronze medals for the winners.

We went through pool play only losing to West team, who beat us convincingly. We won our first playoff match and drew the undefeated West team in the gold-medal match. As we prepared to play, I studied the statistics to see if I could find a way to beat a very good team. We needed an edge. I noticed that the West team rarely set their right-side player – only 2 or 3 times a match. In our last practice before we played for the gold medal, I told the team we were not going to block their right-side attacker but would instead move all our blockers into positions in front of the setter. We would have 3 blockers on 2 hitters – their strongest hitters. I had to do a real sales job on them because they looked at me like I had gone completely crazy. My assistant coach, a guy who coached Division I, thought I was totally nuts and made it very clear to everyone.

When the match started, the first set for the West team went to their right-side player. With no block up against her, she buried it. All the players on the court immediately looked at me. I calmly told them that it was OK and to stick with the plan. Of course, my assistant coach gloated. Briefly. We ended up winning in 2 games and totaled 27 blocks! (In those days, we played 15-point games with no rally scoring.) The most amazing thing was that the other coaches never made any adjustments. Their right-side player had only that one kill in the two games. Of course, they had probably never played anyone who, as the ball was served, lined up with 3 blockers in front of the setter. The moral of the story is, sometimes you have to use creative (maybe even unorthodox) tactics and strategies to beat a better team.

Final Thoughts

I firmly believe coaches should challenge players. But I think we need to do it while treating them with respect, coupled with a humanistic approach. I've never known a player who walks on the court to purposely mess up. I cringe at some of the things I did as a young coach because I thought I needed to be "tough" on the players. Talk to them, find out what is bothering them and try to solve problems together.

For more from Stephanie and
other exceptional volleyball coaches visit
www.theartofcoachingvolleyball.com

About the Author

Seven hundred college wins is reason enough to listen to what Stephanie Schleuder has to say about training the mind for volleyball, but her credentials run deeper. In a career in which she served as head volleyball coach at the University of Minnesota, University of Alabama and Macalester College and was also president of the American Volleyball Coaches Association, Schleuder never just accepted that the way to do something is the way you've always done it. She tweaked and refined and reshaped her philosophy so she could grow as a coach while her athletes grew as volleyball players.

Interestingly, her biggest influence wasn't another coach but, rather, a professor of kinesiology – Dr. Joann Johnson – whom Schleuder took a class from during her junior year at University of Minnesota Duluth. Dr. Johnson's specialty was motor learning, and her students absorbed the subject largely through experimentation – things like trying to write longhand while looking in a mirror.

"Being in her classes lit a fire under me," Schleuder says. "It got me interested in learning how to learn."

Schleuder applied that to volleyball, thinking deeply for many years about how she could best reach student-athletes in ways that would help them become better players and better people. It was often challenging. One time, a player got so annoyed with Schleuder that she threw her backpack at her. But Schleuder didn't give up on her. In fact, she learned from the incident. It made her realize that extreme frustration is often just an indicator of how serious an athlete is about wanting to become great.

In "Brain Training for Volleyball," Schleuder shares methods that have consistently worked for her in practice after practice, match after match, season after season. She covers teaching leadership, building trust, defeating distractions, encouraging a higher level of focus, coaching captains and much more. It's a great read, and it's also a valuable resource for coaches seeking ways to be better prepared for the upcoming season than they were for the previous season.